19, 32, 72, 141, 267

NOTES

including
- *Life and Background*
- *List of Characters*
- *Style and Structure in* Catch-22
- *Critical Commentaries*
- *The Novel and Its Tradition*
- *Review Questions*
- *Selected Bibliography*

by
C. A. Peek, Ph.D.
Assistant Professor of English
Northern Arizona University

INCORPORATED

LINCOLN, NEBRASKA 68501

Editor

Gary Carey, M.A.
University of Colorado

Consulting Editor

James L. Roberts, Ph.D.
Department of English
University of Nebraska

ISBN 0-8220-0296-5
© Copyright 1975
by
Cliffs Notes, Inc.
All Rights Reserved
Printed in U.S.A.

1998 Printing

Cliffs Notes, Inc.   Lincoln, Nebraska

CONTENTS

Catch-22 Notes

LIFE AND BACKGROUND

Joseph Heller was born in Brooklyn, May 1, 1923. He married in 1945, has two children, and now resides in Manhattan. He has a Bachelor of Arts from New York University where he was a Phi Beta Kappa and a Master of Arts from Columbia, and was a Fulbright Scholar at Oxford University. Aside from writing, most of his life has been spent in teaching and journalism, with teaching assignments at Yale, Pennsylvania State University, and City College of New York, and journalistic and advertising positions with *Time, Look,* and *McCalls.* He has also worked on scripts for a television series under the name Max Orange, and has worked on screenplays for motion pictures. He served as a bombardier in the Air Force during World War II and logged over 60 missions. For his personal views, the reader can refer to a number of interviews with Heller in *Intellectual Digest* (December, 1971), *Washington Post* (March 15, 1962), *Book World* (July 21, 1969), *Newsday* (July 23, 1971), and New York *Times* (December 3, 1967).

His two best-known works are a play, *We Bombed in New Haven,* portions of which appeared on National Education Television in The Great American Dream Machine, and this novel, *Catch-22.* The novel has also been dramatized by Heller and was first performed at the John Drew Theater in East Hampton, New York, July 13, 1971, directed by Larry Arrick (who also did *We Bombed in New Haven*).

The dramatized version, excluding the character of Orr and the Eternal City episode and relying heavily on interrogation scenes from the novel, shows Heller's pre-occupation with the abuse of legal processes, a concern which grew with the conspiracy trials of the 1960's but which was fostered even before by the anti-Communist crusades of the 1940's and 1950's.

In addition, Heller has written shorter pieces, including "Catch-22 Revisited" (*Holiday,* 41 (April, 1967), 44-61) and "How I Found James Bond" (*Holiday,* 41 (June, 1967), 123-125), and an excellent book review (*New Republic,* 147 (July 30, 1962), 23-24).

Heller has a new novel, *Something Happened* (Knopf), an earlier section of which appeared in *Esquire* in 1966. Indeed, in its 1963 review of *Catch-22, Time* anticipated the novel appearing in 1964. The excerpt appeared in 1966, and it wasn't until thirteen years after the publication of *Catch-22* that *Something Happened* appeared. The novel traces the impressions of its protagonist, Bob Slocum, in an effort to dramatize the undramatic life of modern man and to probe the personal disorientation which occurs in the face of the collapse of society. This newest creation of Heller is reviewed by John W. Aldridge, "Vision of Man Raging in a Vacuum," *Saturday Review* (October 19, 1974), 18-21.

LIST OF CHARACTERS

Aardvaark (Aarfy)

Yossarian's navigator who pretends he can't hear Yossarian during the bomb runs. Aarfy is later exposed as both cruel and criminal.

Appleby

A member of Yossarian's squadron who angers Orr while playing ping-pong. They refer to him as having flies in his eyes.

Captain Black

The nasty intelligence officer for the squadron who frustrates Nately by procuring Nately's whore.

Colonel Cathcart

A full colonel who wants to be general in Gen. Dreedle's outfit. Col. Cathcart keeps raising the number of missions and fears "black eyes" while hoping for "feathers in his cap."

Clevinger

A member of Yossarian's squadron who has a dopey brain. He conducts the educational sessions, is interrogated by the Action Board, and dies on the Parma bomb run.

Major — de Coverly

The one-eyed procurer of R&R facilities for the officers and enlisted men. His Jehovan bearing puts an end to the Great Loyalty Oath Crusade.

Major Danby

The group operations officer, threatened with being shot by Gen. Dreedle. He later argues with Yossarian over idealism and helps Yossarian to leave.

Doc Daneeka

The medial officer who first explains Catch-22 to Yossarian. He has arranged to be listed on flight schedules, but doesn't fly. His "theme" is "What about me?"

Dobbs
The co-pilot who takes the controls from Huple on the Avignon mission and who proposes Col. Cathcart's assassination.

General Dreedle
The blunt, irascible commander of a wing in the Mediterranean theater of operations.

Nurse Duckett
A ward nurse in the hospital at Pianosa who has a brief affair with Yossarian.

Dunbar
Yossarian's companion in the hospital who tries to make time pass slowly and who is "disappeared" after the second episode with the soldier in white.

Dori Duz
Lt. Scheisskopf's wife's promiscuous friend.

Captain Flume
The officer who shares a trailer with Chief White Halfoat until the Chief threatens to slit his throat and he moves into the woods.

Gus
One of the two enlisted men who run Doc Daneeka's medical tent, whose chief "cure" is painting patients' gums and toes purple.

Chief White Halfoat
The half-blooded Indian from Oklahoma who obligingly punches Col. Moodus in the nose for Gen. Dreedle and who "knows" he will die of pneumonia.

Havermeyer
The lead bombardier who won't take evasive action. He takes Mudd's pistol to his tent next to Yossarian's and shoots field mice.

Huple
Hungry Joe's roommate whose cat eventually kills Hungry Joe. He is the under-aged pilot on the mission to Avignon.

Hungry Joe
The lustful squad member who invents the "famous photographer" line and has nightmares whenever he isn't scheduled to fly.

Colonel Korn

The assistant to Col. Cathcart. He is by far the more clever of the two.

Kraft

The pilot killed over Ferrara on the second run ordered by Yossarian. He wanted "only to be liked."

Luciana

The girl with the scarred back whom Yossarian meets at the Allied Officers' club and "proposes" marriage to.

McWatt

A pilot, first Clevinger's and then Nately's roommate who heedlessly buzzes the squadron, eventually killing Kid Sampson.

Major Major

The squadron commander who will only see people when he is not in to see them.

Milo Minderbinder

The mess officer turned syndicate head who masterminds a black market and bombs his own men for profit.

Colonel Moodus

General Dreedle's hated son-in-law who is taunted by the general's nurse and punched by Chief White Halfoat.

Mudd

The name of the dead man in Yossarian's tent, in turn the reference to a pile of personal belongings eventually tossed out by Yossarian's four new roomies.

Lieutenant Nately

The squadron member from a wealthy home who loves a whore and argues with the diabolical old man. He is killed on the La Spezia mission along with Dobbs.

Orr

Yossarian's "tinkering" roommate who nearly always has to ditch his plane. His successful arrival in Sweden renews Yossarian's faith.

General Peckem

The general in charge of special operations who along with his assistant, Col. Cargill, plots to take over Gen. Dreedle's command.

Kid Sampson
One of Yossarian's pilots. Eventually he is killed by McWatt in a macabre accident.

Lieutenant Scheisskopf
Eventually General Scheisskopf, he begins as the parade-crazy assistant with the promiscuous wife.

Soldier in White
The wholly bandaged body in the hospital asserted to be Lieutenant Schmulker.

Snowden
A squadron gunner who dies in Yossarian's arms as Yossarian patches the wrong wound. His "secret" haunts Yossarian till nearly the end.

Chaplain Tappman
The kindly chaplain who befriends Yossarian. He is full of doubts and fears, but overcomes them in the end.

Wes
The other of the two medics working under Doc Daneeka.

Corporal Whitcomb
The chaplain's antagonistic and atheistic assistant who starts the letter of condolence game and is responsible for the CID investigation of the chaplain.

ex-PFC Wintergreen
The continually promoted and then busted mail clerk at Twenty-seventh Air Force Headquarters who virtually runs the 27th by intercepting messages and forging answers.

Yossarian
Yossarian receives most of the attention of the novel, both as a captain in the squadron, a bombardier on the flights, and a culprit/victim of catch-22.

STYLE AND STRUCTURE IN CATCH-22

To the reader who regards style as mere adornment and structure as mere form, *Catch-22* must appear a frustratingly jumbled series of disconnected episodes. The novel is written, however, within the viewpoint that style and structure limit and condition what is and what can be said.

Structurally, the reader needs to be aware of how the novel is organized and unified. The organizing principle of the novel is not chronology. Time is disjointed, and episodes are placed for one of two purposes. The first of these purposes is to juxtapose two scenes in order to show their relevance to one another, regardless of their chronological order. For example in the beginning and middle of chapter two, Yossarian is arguing with Clevinger, but in between we are shown where Yossarian lives at a time when Clevinger "had still not returned." The purpose of this rapid juxtaposition is to establish an ironic perspective on Clevinger's claim that war is impersonal. Another example of this is the lifting of the first chapter out of sequence in order to establish the importance of the hospital, the friendship of Yossarian and the chaplain, and the psychology of Yossarian from the outset.

The second criterion for the placement of episodes is the requirement that they create a graduated series of events. For example, we are given several interrogation scenes, each more sinister than the one before. Or we see several attempts at a bomb run, each new attempt heightening the psychological impact on the men.

In disjointing time in this way, the structure contributes to the content of the novel where time equals mortality and, therefore, disjoints the lives of men in the squadron. And, without this structure, the presentation of the theme of *deja vu,* the sensation of having seen something before, would be impossible.

Nevertheless, these seemingly disjointed series can be followed chronologically due, again, to a structural device, the repetition of three key incidents. The recurring reference to Snowden's death scene, the continuing growth of M and M enterprises, and the raising of the number of missions all provide focal points for the organization of the novel and, in turn, provide much of the motivation for the action of the story.

This structure is abetted and maintained by the novel's style. In part, the style is that of satire, using exaggerations, grotesque and comic caricatures, and telling allusions. But what, for example, is exaggerated on a literal level is all too true on, for instance, the psychological level; and the style makes possible the novel's emphasis on and attention to just that and other analogous levels. In line with the satiric style, note the naming of characters for comic effect; for examples, Scheisskopf, meaning "shithead"; the appellation "Hungry" for Joe; and Danby, with its echoes of namby-pamby, for the middle-aged idealist major.

Apart from the satiric style, two other styles can be identified. The first of these is the descriptive style. Doc Daneeka, "roosted dolorously like a shivering turkey buzzard"; the mountains, blanketed in a "mesmerizing quiet," Yossarian, wet "with the feeling of warm slime," "lavender gloom clouding the entrance of the operations tent"; the style serves to transcend physical reality both by making sensations metaphors for states of mind and by attributing unusual qualities to objects, making the reader take a second look at familiar objects and feelings. Consistent with this, the descriptions oftentimes become totally surrealistic, abandoning realism altogether, as in the portraits of voluptuousness in the Rome apartment or the description of Yossarian's walk through the Eternal City. And this, too, serves to "overthrow" the reader's preconceptions, allowing the novel to develop the theme of increased, new and altered perceptions of the world.

The second of these styles is that employed in the dialogue, particularly the comic dialogue. Because both the comedy and the dialogue in the novel revolve around conflicts in perspectives, much of the dialogue takes the form of an altercation or disputation. When such dialogues take the form of alternating retorts, each not much more than a word or a line and playing on the opponents' own words, this is called stichomythia, and the style of such dialogue in *Catch-22* is often stichomythic. This style dominates such dialogues as the arguments between Clevinger and Orr and the interrogation of Clevinger. In the former case there are even elaborations on this in which the opposing line is inserted mid-way in the line of the protagonist, as for example:

> Yossarian: He was —
> Clevinger: Crazy...
> Yossarian: — immense.

This style of dialogue accomplishes a dual goal; it makes it possible for the author to raise two distinct lines of thought while at the same time casting doubt on both lines and on the clarity of those who argue for each line. Thus, while the reader can see issues being drawn, the characters are often left befuddled. In this way the stichomythia creates the context for the novel's investigation of alternative ideas about life. As Orr is already present with the men so are the alternatives imbedded in their own thinking. This lends itself to the exploitation of this stylistic device which employs an opponent's own words against him.

Thus the style itself always suggests that there is more than meets the eye, and this in turn is not only a theme of the novel but the necessary framework for breaking out of the cynical, materialistic hedonism which pervades the mentality of the characters and locks the characters in a world barren of courage and hope.

CRITICAL COMMENTARY

CHAPTER ONE

Although the surface of chapter one is simple, this appearance is quite deceiving. The reader should note the details of time, place, and character in these early chapters, because *Catch-22* develops, in plot and in theme, by the continual re-occurrence of these elements in new and different situations, each new context adding to and elaborating on ideas until their meaning becomes more fully realized, both by the reader and by the characters themselves.

In chapter one, not only are the characters themselves important, but so also are the contrasts in character and the overall irony of the chapter. Note particularly the setting: the hospital in Pianosa. Yossarian's trips to the hospital will become more and more important as the novel progresses. The hospital, which we might associate negatively with sickness and positively with health, is here associated positively with escape and negatively with one of the major themes of the novel: insanity. Note how Yossarian and the chaplain talk about who is crazy and sane and how the sanest ward in the hospital becomes "the only sane ward in the whole world."

The irony is present here in such remarks as the comment that the Texan is so good-natured that no one can stand him and that Nately got off to a bad start in life by coming from a good family. These ironic elements will grow in the course of the novel until they are significant thematically, and so will personal characterizations, such as the Texan's racism and, especially, the chaplain's ineptitude.

One other element initiated here and used by Heller as a significant device throughout the novel is the device of literary allusion. Here, for instance, we have the allusion to *Moby Dick,* which the "pedantic cetologist," a victim of fate himself, wants to discuss with the "dying colonel," and those who have read *Moby Dick* should remember that death and predestiny are two of the themes of the novel alluded to.

Finally, readers should note the religious theme developed in casual comments, characterizations, and allusions, such as the narrator's description of Yossarian's flick of the wrist as he signs Washington Irving's name as being done "as though he were God."

CHAPTER TWO

This chapter begins with explicit reminders of the two "worlds" the characters must choose between: the hospital and the war outside. Clevinger and Yossarian proceed to argue on the subject of sanity carried over from chapter one. Since Clevinger argues from the perspective of the war and Yossarian argues from the perspective of the hospital, they are constantly at cross purposes. The argument and the chapter, however, do serve to acquaint the reader with more of Yossarian's attitudes; and we begin to associate Yossarian with the concept of *life* as opposed to Clevinger and others who are associated with *principles.*

Two elements are introduced here which grow to be of central importance later. The first of these is Milo's mess hall operation which will develop larger and larger symbolic overtones. The other is the number of missions to be flown. This will not only provide a motive force for much of the action of the novel, but, together with the growth of Milo's operations, will provide a time clue for the chronology of the novel. Note also that Dunbar's ruse to make time pass more slowly (an elaborate pun on the meaning of time) and the presence of the CID are again mentioned in this chapter.

CHAPTER THREE

This chapter should alert the reader to the way in which the novel works both structurally and stylistically (and thematically as well since thematic development is tied to style and structure here). For instance there is the abrupt change in time and place, from Pianosa at the time of Yossarian's release from the hospital to Rome at an earlier time. This shift is accomplished through the common recollections of Orr and Yossarian — the extent to which Orr and Yossarian think alike will become more important as the novel progresses — and the purpose of the shift is to set two scenes side by side to enable the reader to begin to see the thematic significance of each scene in a way that would be impossible if the scenes were separated by intervening material. Yossarian's conversation with Orr is also a good example of the way in which language games work in the novel, creating through puns and distortions of context an enigma to be puzzled over.

These games are abetted by two other devices of the novel, exaggeration and reversal, as in the case of the self-made Col. Cargill "who owed his lack of success to nobody." This chapter also serves to suggest how decisions are made and by whom, an issue which will be raised repeatedly to call those decisions into question. This questioning of decisions will be a major distinction between the two outlooks represented by Clevinger and Yossarian in the last chapter and continued by Havermeyer and Yossarian in this one. The idea of life advanced by Yossarian is also contrasted here with the shooting of the mice, and from this point on there will be many oblique comparisons of men and mice or rats. But note how Heller keeps these comparisons from lapsing into the "man or mouse" cliché.

There is a brief allusion in this chapter to a central event of the novel, the bombing of the squadron by Milo; and this foreshadowing is just enough to upset the comic tone of these early chapters. This more serious vein is also suggested in the narrator's description, "ignorant armies clashed by night," an allusion to Arnold's "Dover Beach," and the suggestion culminates here in the macabre image of "tongueless dead men" who people the "night hours like living ghosts." The reader will find it helpful later to have made a mental note of such references to ghosts and specters.

All the while, the predominant feature of this chapter is the enigmatic figure of Orr, and readers should watch his development and activity carefully.

CHAPTER FOUR

The main point of this chapter is emphasized in the final question, "What else is there?" In other words, the chapter portrays a number of people principally concerned with themselves and their life and happiness and asks, is there anything but this? And, although there is no answer to this question immediately forthcoming, the chapter does raise questions about the machinations we go through in the interest of these "ideals."

Using Doc Daneeka as a pivotal point, the chapter raises the issues of the use of talents and brains, the place of questioning ideas and traditions, and the worth of a long but meaningless life. Principally, through Yossarian's humorous misunderstanding of Doc Daneeka's catch phrase, "You scratch my back, I'll scratch yours," this chapter questions the philosophy of getting ahead through mutual favors, a philosophy which is disavowed quickly even by its principal proponent, the Doc.

Against this age-old, accepted idea of the way to live, the chapter raises the possibility inherent in questioning life. The questioning sessions, however, are cancelled not only because of the ingenious formula regarding who can ask questions, but also because the only question really asked is the same as Doc Daneeka's question, "Why me?" It is in this connection that the novel asserts the necessity of a re-education of our perceptions if the question at the end of the chapter, what else is there?, is to have an answer; but the chapter also indicates the impossibility of educating those who won't question any of the "givens" of their existence. In the absence of any questions except "Why me?", the only course seems to be Dunbar's, the extension of life by whatever means possible. Note here how time is defined in terms of age and age is defined, in turn, as proximity to death. Within the logic of those definitions, Dunbar's stretching of time seems to be an irrefutable course; and only a re-definition will allow the reader and characters to provide an answer to Dunbar's question. In the meantime, Dunbar's strategems and the terrors of existence read like a catalogue drawn from Schopenhauer's pessimism in *The World as Will and Idea,* and in one way, this novel can be seen as an answer to Schopenhauer.

Thus the business of skeet shooting makes sense in these terms, even though it is obviously senseless: "Shooting skeet...it was excellent training...it trained them to shoot skeet." The reader should pay careful attention, however, to the contrasts in character given in this chapter, for each contrast suggests a possible perspective on this issue.

Readers might also notice how Wintergreen is able to disturb or influence people by a casually dropped word and how this relates to the discussion in the previous chapter of how decisions are made.

CHAPTER FIVE

The discussion of perception, raised in chapter four, is carried on in chapter five by the humor of the flies in Appleby's eyes. This discussion leads to the contrast drawn between flies in the eyes and crumbs on the chin—that is, perception versus material satisfaction. In this chapter, too, this issue is elevated to the traditional concern of literature and philosophy, the distinction between appearance and reality. The extent of this concern is evident in the ultimate contrast between the "cosmological wickedness" which jars the plane and the sunlight always present as it turns toward the target. Within this horrifying reality, however, we find many of the characters actually welcomed the war: "Luckily, the war broke out just in the nick of time." Twice in this chapter this idea is given expression, first by Doc Daneeka and, second, by Chief White Halfoat.

Out of the contrast of appearance and reality comes the paradox of Catch-22, and the definition of that catch given in this chapter is all the more significant for being stated in terms of one of the major themes, craziness and sanity. Despite the logical appearance of the catch, however, it fails to answer the question "Why?" which is constantly being raised only to be frustrated. Thus the men continue to live in fear, and this chapter emphasizes fear as one of the chief things which matter. Somehow the material benefits of the war are unable to overcome the overwhelming anxiety experienced by most of the men.

This whole experience of fear and anxiety finds expression in chapter five in the metaphor of the B-25, in its design at once a womb and a tomb, the inept placement of the escape crawlway—which should provide comfort—leading only to further anxiety. This metaphor in turn becomes a metaphor for life itself, extended as it is by the reference, once again, to the way in which a man, in this case in the crawlway, is like a "yellow-bellied rat."

The fear and anxiety depicted here are increased by the realization that what had been passed on as wisdom by teachers, relatives, and lawmakers, was really a lie. Even within the bleakness of the picture drawn by this chapter, however, the novel is true to its satiric form, suggesting by contrast what virtues (for example, Truth) are at the basis of the vision of the author and hold the promise, if realized, of making a reformation possible. In this sense, much of the novel deals with the traditional question of how virtue can be realized in a world that is terrifyingly vicious.

Note here, too, how these themes are aided by the descriptive technique, shown at its best in the depiction of the B-25 flight. Here one adjective builds on the previous adjectives until the purely physical sensations are increased to psychological proportions and the suggestion of apocalypse. This technique is made all the more effective by the continuous interweaving of stories, particularly seen in this chapter in the various stories of the young couple who visited Doc Daneeka, the affinity of Chief White Halfoat's family for finding oil, the flies in Appleby's eyes, the flight, and the recurrent suggestion of a story behind the mere mention of the Snowden incident.

CHAPTER SIX

Once again the number of required missions is increased in this chapter, but here the number of missions serves as a backdrop for the reference to several deaths; and it becomes more clear that illogic and absurdity have their price in human lives. These violent deaths are underscored by the violence which lies just under the surface of day-to-day life and breaks out now and again in such episodes as Orr's attack on Appleby.

The violence and absurdity of the situation lead to the phenomenon of Hungry Joe's "inverted set of responses," the nightmares. These nightmares constitute an inverted response, however, only within certain perspectives; and these perspectives are challenged here. In fact, it is suggested that just possibly this response is the sensible one. This is not to say, however, that Hungry Joe is not "sick," as the narrator asserts at the beginning of the chapter; and one manifestation of his ailment is the ludicrous sensuality of his extreme hedonism. In Hungry Joe's continuing pursuit of sexual gratification, the novel raises the traditional theme of *carpe diem* — the idea that pursuit of pleasure is the only meaning to be found in the face of our mortality. In this chapter this theme is given added force by the suggestion that God is negligent, guilty of cosmic oversights, and of resting while men die. This theme will be developed later in the form of a full-fledged theological debate.

In the meantime, the illogic typical of the exercise of power and the absurd way in which decisions are made is emphasized through the growing revelation of the key role played by Wintergreen, summed up by his use of "we" to describe his own relationship to established power. Furthermore, this chapter suggests the motive behind the phenomenon of staying on the right side of power by not rocking the boat: fear for our personal well-being. "If you're going to be shot," asks Wintergreen rhetorically, "whose side do you expect me to be on?"

This time, the definition of Catch-22 is given in terms of power and authority, in keeping with the general theme of the chapter. Again, however, the new definition fails to satisfy, and the only answer given here to "Why?," as in Captain Flume's anxious question to Chief White Halfoat, is the Chief's answer, "Why not?"

CHAPTER SEVEN

Note that this chapter begins, once again, with a discussion of craziness and sanity, this time in the context of amazement at one who is apparently sane and yet can tolerate the war.

Relevant to this discussion is the novel's first overture into Milo's operation. Here we find the first details, however scant and puzzling, of Milo's deals. These deals are based on the principle of "self" or "me first," although they are cloaked with the motto, "everyone has a share" (possibly a reference to President Roosevelt's insistence about our National Debt, "we owe it to ourselves"). It is supposedly this sharing which makes Milo's operations a syndicate, but it is really the double dealing made possible by the double talk which makes the syndicate possible. The chapter ends, incidentally, with a hint as to another of Milo's deals, replete with enigma and contradiction.

Imbedded in this episode is the reference to Milo's eyesight, a reference which parallels that of the flies in Appleby's eyes. In this case, however, Milo sees "more things than most people," but "none of them too distinctly." What we have, in other words, is a clash between Milo's enterprising aggressiveness and Yossarian's evasiveness...thus they are mutually unable to understand one another. Milo's own "game" conflicts with Yossarian's game, in that Milo wants to provide the best and most healthy food available and Yossarian's game is to eat only those foods which will send him back to the hospital.

Nevertheless, Milo is shrewd. Although his failure to see "too distinctly" discredits him as the absolute authority, Milo knows the bases of human character with which he must deal. Therefore, it is important to note Milo's immediate trust of Yossarian and the basis for that trust.

It might be well to notice, too, the conjunction of the mention of the black market—and Milo's interest in that—and of Milo's rigid principles, principles conveniently adopted, to be sure, but held with something very similar to moral conviction. In other words, Milo rationalizes so effectively that he is able to convince at least himself—and often others—that his way is the right way, the "socially responsible" way.

CHAPTER EIGHT

In this chapter, Clevinger's hearing bears much resemblance to the rationale for Milo's operations, both existing as they do on the basis of misuse of the meaning of words. The trial revolves around the theory that being accused means there must be some guilt. This trial culminates, however, in the serious question, "What is justice?," the Socratic question underlying both law and philosophy.

Here the confusions are multiplied because, once again, they are buttressed by the difference between appearance and reality. This is accentuated by the blatant acknowledgment of the difference between the estimation and the actual capacity of Clevinger's intelligence in itself and as applied to the situation of Lt. Scheisskopf's appeal, "I *want* someone to tell me," another case of the difference between appearance and reality.

The reader could well note the business about Lt. Scheisskopf's parades, for here the parades, as so much else in the novel, are a metaphor, this time for all sorts of routine busywork and particularly for the kind of mentality behind that busywork. So, for such parades, the awards become victories without triumphs.

Throughout the chapter we find Yossarian in love, with Dori Duz, Lt. Scheisskopf's wife, or with whomever is present. This promiscuity sheds doubt on the reality of his love, however real it is on the basis of feelings alone, and is heightened by the concluding comments on Clevinger's amazement at the hate he sees and the need for real love in the affairs of this microcosmic world of Pianosa. Thus, Love joins Truth as another of the virtues the novel will ultimately uphold.

CHAPTER NINE

Chapter nine begins with another literary allusion, this time to Edward Arlington Robinson's "Miniver Cheevy," a poem about the discrepancy between appearance and reality; and this is just one more part of the prodigious effort of the author to keep this theme continually before the reader's mind. Here it is abetted by the reversal of the cliché about greatness thrust upon one; totally opposite to this is Major Major, who has mediocrity thrust upon him. Thus, Heller is able to debunk the cliché at the same time that he emphasizes the quality of Major Major's life.

The beginning of Major Major's life is a lie — one will remember Yossarian's and Chief White Halfoat's recollections of being lied to as children — and this lie has to do with his very identity — his name. Subsequently, he experiences rejection. It should be noted that, no matter how comic the situation proposed by the novel, it is true to psychological reality. In this case, the reality is being the rejected stranger as a boy or youth or young man because of some personal peculiarity, something many young people experience.

The anonymity of Major Major, however, is almost predestined, a fact accentuated indirectly both by the reference to his father's "Calvinism" and by the inclusion of his story in a chapter whose substance, for the most part, rests in the repetition of events: Major — de Coverly's horseshoe playing, the Ferrara incident, the episode of the naked man, and the signing of Washington Irving's name. Each of these episodes is alluded to frequently, not only to maintain the reader's attention to them but also to jade that attention—that is, to render these episodes commonplace and, thus, lessen in the overall scheme than the characters think at the time.

The promotion of Major Major, however, fits nicely into the theme of who decides what and why, a theme which, along with the reaction to his peculiarities, is accentuated by his scheme for being left alone, another example in itself of the double talk which these people resort to to save themselves. The reader might well follow these attempts to see if any of them ultimately succeed.

The chapter ends, again, on the theme of "whose side are you on, boys"; and, again, the only answer Yossarian can give is that it is a damn fool who is not on the side of the majority—that is, the winning side.

CHAPTER TEN

The "disappearance" of Clevinger suggests how little individual human beings count in the world depicted by the novel. This is a theme which will be pursued later in these same terms. In such a world, Wintergreen and his holes are, indeed, wisdom. Here, Wintergreen personifies the anti-hero of modern literature, the man with no loyalties to anything higher than himself. Thus he is able to play the novel's language game, ascribing his escape from duty as duty in itself, one which he performs better than others perform theirs.

In the wake of this, Appleby goes away from Major Major's headquarters very confused by the double-talk there, and immediately there is a recollection of the atabrine episode. This recollection may call to the reader's mind Yossarian's comment about knowing they were sick but not knowing they were poisoned. In this same vein the novel plays off "tricks" versus "purpose" in the argument that closes the chapter. This, in turn, is supplemented by the subject of "Mudd," a victim of chance, which we know from a previous chapter means circumstance (which Yossarian opposes vehemently), the opposite of purpose.

Once again, however, these phenomenon are not meant to be seen as being isolated to Pianosa. Mention of the family of man enlarges the scope of Pianosa, and this reference is recapitulated in the idea that the world is a charnel house, an idea which makes it clear that the novel is not dealing with just a locality but the human predicament. This total predicament is underscored by the continued repetition of incidents.

The chapter ends with the return to the issue of craziness and insanity, this time with the suggestion that, once again, appearances may be deceiving, and that craziness may in fact be the sane path. This thought is given a further dimension by such descriptive phrases as "sulphurous fog," giving the connotation of the brimstone we associate with the hellish and satanic, thus raising the issue to cosmic proportions.

CHAPTER ELEVEN

The Glorious Loyalty Oath Crusade gives the reader a taste of Heller's satire. On one level what is satirized is the super-patriotism of those who think allegiance to one's country can be forced and who define loyalty in terms of superficial acts. Heller gives us the distorted logic that no one who is loyal would object to proving it by signing pledges, and he shows the distortion by carrying that logic to its consequence: the more you sign the more loyal you are—it doesn't even matter whether you mean it or not. Note, too, how Captain Black confuses adults expressing their commitments with children learning the meaning of allegiance.

The satire on super-patriotism operates on a higher level, however, as a satire against dominating bureaucracy in general as the squadron begins to realize that the administrators whose job is to serve them have taken control of their lives instead. Appropriately, it is Major——de Coverly who puts an end to the crusade. Here he is described as having a "Jehovan bearing," and we are told that the "wall" of officers parts before him like the Red Sea, a reference to Moses' deliverance of the Hebrew people. The injection of a Godlike figure here picks up on the allusion to Jehovah in chapter two.

Besides setting a framework for the squadron's deliverance from the crusade, however, this build-up of Major——de Coverly prepares the way for the comic deflation of expectations which occurs when the supposedly suave and indomitable major orders, "Gimme eat." Despite the deflation, however, the major—who really does affect his world—contrasts with Captain Black who can only pretend to be "a man of real consequence" through the imposition of his will in pseudo causes.

CHAPTER TWELVE

Chapter twelve begins with the men waiting in the rain and ends with the rain ceasing. This not only establishes rain as a metaphor, but allows the introduction of Hungry Joe's dream as a metaphor, too. In between are scenes of the moving of the bomb line, Wintergreen's competition with Milo, the recurring argument between Clevinger and Yossarian, the story of the La Page glue gun, and the drunk scene. How are these to be understood?

First, Heller helps us through the context of style. The punning description of Nately's "grave young face" sets the tone for the chapter, a tone broken by comic action. This comedy is aided by the repetition of lines, particularly those concerning Peckem's "ability to get men to agree." This device, however, alerts us to the device of juxtaposition which dominates the "theological" discussion: each time someone takes the name of

God in vain, it is the occasion for the remark that "There is no God."

Appropriately, this theological discussion is preceded and introduced by another argument between Clevinger and Yossarian over, again, "Why me?," but this time placed in a discussion of rationality and superstition. We are to understand, however, that neither side is "right" in terms of the novel: Clevinger, the rationalist, is to die; and Yossarian's "knocking on wood" and "crossing his fingers" are thwarted by the ending of the rain.

The language games, seen earlier, are being used here in Yossarian's question-begging response, "It doesn't make a damned bit of difference *who* wins the war to someone who's dead." The response evades the issue of what difference it might make to the same man while living (and also assumes death to be a state of unconsciousness). In other words, both rationality and superstition are seen here to be alternative responses to fear of the end of one's existence.

These alternatives dispensed with, we are ready to see Hungry Joe's dream of suffocation as a metaphor for the human condition. The dream is, we note, irrepressible; and its being framed by the drunk scene and the "duel" between Joe and the cat is understandable – that is, it is understandable why these men, like those in *M*A*S*H*, are "avid for any diversion."

CHAPTER THIRTEEN

Beginning, as it does, immediately subsequent to the closing event of the last chapter, and moving to different times – those of the episode in Rome, the scene of Milo and the egg, and the raid on Ferrara – this chapter offers a good example of the disjointed time operating in the novel. Far from being simply a stylistic device, this disjuncture is here representative of the disjointed lives of the men themselves, lives held, as described here, in the "dilemma of duty and damnation."

Again, Major — de Coverly provides a perspective on what follows, setting up a contrast between his effect on his world and the ineffectuality of the others. The Jehovan metaphor seen earlier is continued here as we find him described as "eternally indestructible" and as "a Colossus." This metaphor is deepened by the fact that his loss of one eye is attributed to a man described as being "like Satan himself." Note that, like God, Major — de Coverly rules by fiat: he calls Milo the mess officer and, presto, Milo is the mess officer.

And, again too, the chapter takes up the theme of reality and appearance in its discussion of the motives behind Yossarian's medal and promotion. In depicting Col. Korn's reasoning, "to act boastfully about something we ought to be ashamed of," as the basest kind of motivation, the novel satirizes our concern for appearances. And this satire is heightened by contrast with Yossarian's real sense of guilt for having "killed

Kraft and his crew."

Yossarian, nevertheless, is caught up in this concern. He considers his part in the raid as a participation in the same "vile, excruciating dilemma," and this is the source of his guilt. At this point, however, he is confusing acts he can be responsible for with consequences which are beyond his control. This confusion is highlighted by his willing cooperation in Col. Korn's and Col. Cathcart's scheme, something for which he really can be held accountable. In other words, Yossarian has yet to develop an individual perspective and is, thus, susceptible to outside influences, as Major — de Coverly is not. But it is his acquiescence, not his bravery, that really put him "up to his own ass" in it.

CHAPTER FOURTEEN

This chapter gives us a sharp reversal in tone. It begins with Yossarian having learned his lesson: no more bravery. But, is that the right lesson to have learned?

First we are led to believe it is by the description of his bombing run and the jubilation when Yossarian's plane turns back. This is heightened by the tension of fear during the run. Descriptive style leads us to this, too, with graver descriptions of Nately in his earphones as being in a "bulky dungeon," of feelings of desolation, of a sense of a "ponderous, primeval lull," and of the "necrotic profusion" of the ominous mushrooms.

But, ironically, the chapter has implicitly prepared us for doubting that Yossarian is on the right track; from start to finish, this is a chapter of reversals. We have at the outset Yossarian's sense of reversal, "Something was terribly wrong if everything was all right." And, true to the course plotted by that compass, we come to the final reversal, "Bologna was a milk run." Thus, again, doubts are raised about appearances. And the reader would do well to note that with regard to the little incident Heller submerges in this narrative, the reference to Orr and the ditching of his plane; whatever it means at this point, that ditching action contrasts, in its implied bravery, with Yossarian's action, an action typified by Doc Daneeka's "poignant solicitude for his own safety."

CHAPTER FIFTEEN

This chapter would seem, on its surface, to be rather straightforward. For once we have few diversions; the story is told directly. But, again, the surface is a little misleading, since we begin the chapter with the reversal of reversals — Bologna has to be bombed again.

Here, Heller is using the device called the gradated series. First we have the story of the anticipated bomb run, then the first run, then the "real" run. This series is what Yossarian is describing when he says he feels "dulled, lured, trapped." Very often, this device ends in an anti-climax, as it does here as Orr, who ditched his plane in the last chapter, only crash-lands it in this one.

With regard to Orr, note, in order, Aarfy's idea of what happened to Orr, what we expect from the last chapter, and the somewhat ambiguous actuality of Orr's "landing." And note, too, how, swept up in the prevailing sentiment, Yossarian refers to him as a "buck-toothed rat," keeping in mind how "rat" and "mouse" are used as metaphors.

There is one further thing of importance here: the growing frustration between the "men" and the "leaders" has become increasingly evident as an internal frustration as well, as we see exhibited in the quarrel between Aarfy and Yossarian during the run. Yossarian's control of the plane, however, is not part of this pattern. During the bomb runs, including the approach, the bombs away, and the "retreat," the bombardier is in control of the plane; thus, we have Yossarian's orders to McWatt, as we have seen before.

CHAPTER SIXTEEN

Chapter sixteen takes off from Yossarian's decision in chapter fifteen to go to Rome. Part of the irony of the chapter, as we might expect, is that the leave offers Yossarian no rest at all.

In its way, chapter sixteen is the start of one more phase of the novel and, therefore, takes up once again the confusion between love and sex we noted close to the beginning. Here, Yossarian is "in love," but with almost any and every girl he sees. First there is Luciana, then the girl with Aarfy, then the maid "in the lime-colored panties." We discover that Yossarian really is in love — with sex and, even more, with escape. Thus, frustrated by the news that the number of missions has been raised again (this time to 40), he runs to the hospital, now firmly established as an asylum or sanctuary, just as, thwarted in his efforts to find Luciana, he ran to the maid.

In contrast to the light, bantering conversations in this chapter, comic in their circular course, Yossarian is callous, confused, and terrified. Yossarian tears up the slip with Luciana's address, true to her prediction, only to regret it later. Parallel to this, Hungry Joe, allied with Yossarian by their joint condemnation of Aarfy, so loses track of himself that he even tries his "heap big photographer" line on Luciana.

Note, however, that Yossarian is beginning to be able to catch sight of himself in others' eyes, and his desperation is due, in part, to what he is beginning to see.

CHAPTER SEVENTEEN

True to the new beginning made in the previous chapter, chapter seventeen not only carries on the same episode but begins with the same words. Even more, in introducing again the "soldier in white," chapter seventeen makes this new beginning parallel the opening of the book: we are back at the opening scene, but this time with some background; and that allows a somewhat different forward movement.

For example, we find in this chapter how Yossarian came to the idea that everyone is "out to get him," his argument in one of the novel's early "debates." Then true to a "logic" with which we are now becoming familiar, this idea is next reduced to its simplest form: Doc Daneeka's "What about me?"

We are able to see now, however, that the adequacy of the hospital as a refuge is only relative to what is going on outside it; it is only satisfactory at all in the face of the catastrophes lurking everywhere. These catastrophes and their lesser and more comic counterpoints are dubbed "acts of God" (as in insurance policies), but this cliché becomes a somewhat serious discussion of what the men perceive to be the injustice of life which undermines "confidence in this universe."

The catastrophe which we see increasingly referred to is Snowden's death, a pivotal element in *Catch-22*; and that death, even though yet to be seen in detail, provides a perspective on the "mission against mortality." We are being led to ask once again, if we cannot escape mortality, if that is a doomed mission, is there any other mission worthwhile and possible?

CHAPTER EIGHTEEN

This chapter brings us to the heart of both structure and theme in its episode of the man who sees everything twice. First we see this as simply another ruse used to remain in the hospital. Then it is given an added dimension as a pun—not, as one would expect, seeing double, but seeing two of whatever quantity.

This "double vision" prepares the way for the idea of *deja vu,* the sensation of having seen something once before. And the reader might note the closeness of theme and structure as he finds the novel creating just such a sensation itself.

But, as well as structural, this "seeing everything twice" is part of the theme of our perceptiveness, just as were the flies in Appleby's eyes and the continual reference to the eyes of Major—de Coverly. In other words, are there two ways for these men to perceive their world?

This episode is followed immediately by the basic issue to be perceived: the problem of pain—how are we to take the existence of pain and suffering in our world? Here Yossarian and Lt. Scheisskopf's wife argue in what is a parody of the classic theological debates on this subject (Augustine, *City of God;* C. S. Lewis, *The Problem of Pain;* or Dostoevsky, *The Brothers Karamazov*). This argument, through another language game, raises the question of what really constitutes belief and disbelief: the reader might well try to sort out the logical implications of not believing in a good God (Lt. Scheisskopf's wife) and not believing in a bad God (Yossarian).

This chapter does not resolve this debate. Once again, instead, it provides us with the context within which the debate is to be understood. And, once again, the subject of that subsequent episode—the visit to Yossarian by Giuseppe's family—is death. (By continuing to insist on seeing things in the face of the fact of death, the novel can be viewed as existential. In the doctor's insistence that "We're all dying," we have an explicit rejection of the "mission against mortality"; and, in his comment upon illusions, there is a suggestion that, perhaps, we not only don't see things twice, but really don't see things at all, at least not as they are. As evidence, we have the visit in which a family apparently can't distinguish a stranger from their own son.

But, at this point, it is possible the reader will be caught in the illusion. "What difference does it make," asks Giuseppe's mother. "He's dying."

CHAPTER NINETEEN

This chapter centers around Col. Cathcart's play to make publicity and, in consequence, to become a general. On one level it is a study in ambition and the lengths to which ambition can lead, and thus we see a colonel "who calculated day and night in the service of himself." He is a fine example of the observation that a man without character must have a method. His only interest is himself. He adds one more dimension to the novel's study of what happens when self-concern is paramount. And paradoxically this leaves him at the mercy of everyone's opinion of him. Just as Yossarian is beginning to see himself in others' eyes, so Col. Cathcart can see in no other way.

The novel credits this inability (and the subsequent anxiety about "feathers in his cap" and "black eyes") to his being "impervious to absolutes." As an example of this we are given the episode with Col. Cathcart and the chaplain where we see him using religion for his own ends, and his abuse here is a satire on the prevalent forms of using religion in a self-serving manner.

First there is a satire of a religion which offers only comfort (here, a tight bomb pattern) without demands. Secondly, we see a satire on a religion as a civic or social prop (atheism and un-American activity). And, third, we see a satire on a religion used as a matter of social status (the question of admitting the enlisted men). Note here how Heller parodies a standard racial joke—"some of my best friends are Negroes"—in his treatment of Cathcart's view of the enlisted men.

Note, too, how the very name of Yossarian is beginning to create alarm, as it does in the final conversation of the colonel and the chaplain.

CHAPTER TWENTY

Chapter twenty presents us with a psychological study of the chaplain. Although it is entitled "Corporal Whitcomb," the corporal serves here mainly as the epitome of the world within which the chaplain tries to live and work. The study begins with his sense of cowardice, passes to his anxiety about the animosity he seems to provoke, and ends with his tragic sense of ineptitude. While the chaplain takes full responsibility for all of this, part of the purpose of the study is to ask to what extent he really is, or can be, responsible for the unhappiness in the world; and we see that at least part of his sense of guilt stems from swallowing whole, somewhat as does Col. Cathcart, the opinion of others who are generally occupied with pointing out "one of the things wrong" with him. In not being aggressive, ambitious, and calculating, however, he is distinctly unlike Col. Cathcart and Col. Korn and their miniature, Corporal Whitcomb.

The chapter also serves to address openly the *deja vu* theme, prepared for by the earlier episode of the soldier who saw everything twice. And here, the occasion for the chaplain's interest in *deja vu* is alluded to: the case of the naked man at Snowden's funeral.

Also, this chapter is the occasion for another episode of CID investigation. Note how the seemingly innocent episode related in chapter one (the signing of Washington Irving's name) is beginning to have more significant repercussions.

CHAPTER TWENTY-ONE

Here we are given one further dimension of Col. Cathcart's total reliance upon how others see him: he never is sure just how they do see him; and, therefore, he can only project his own anxieties onto them. It is no wonder that he receives no assurance from this, and his situation is highlighted by his counting himself among the "sophisticated, self-assured people."

Using what has been established in the last two chapters as a framework, this chapter goes on to relate several episodes (General Dreedle's treatment of Col. Moodus, the awarding of the Distinguished Flying Cross to Yossarian, and the Avignon briefing), each of which furthers the occasion for advancing some of the themes of the novel.

The discussion of Col. Cathcart's "farm" offers us the ludicrous spectacle of a point-of-view that can rationalize any immoral practice into a legal act. The chapter then writes this in larger letters, as we see a similar justification made by Milo for bombing the group: the bombing made "a huge net profit." With this, we see that not only is war a business (Dreedle takes "his son-in-law into the business"), but also the military setting is now a metaphor for a larger arena: the industrial-financial complex.

In keeping with the larger and larger scope of the novel's concern (eventually, Pianosa stands for the world, and the squad equals mankind), Cathcart sees the trouble he may be in as an "inscrutable cosmic climax." Once the cosmic arena has been suggested, we are next given, true to the associations the novel has been cultivating, Major — de Coverly, the "cosmic" figure.

The chapter then contrasts two episodes, the award presentation in which General Dreedle takes a surprisingly lax view of Yossarian's nakedness, stemming from his lack of shame and pretense, and the Avignon briefing in which we see the callousness which stems from Dreedle's confusion of ideals worth fighting for with the idiosyncrasies of his own superiors. (Note here the device of close repetition used in the presentation of General Dreedle's orders to shoot Major Danby.)

In the main, this chapter, following upon some rather more somber chapters, serves to re-emphasize the comic and humorous as part of the continuing counterpoint of the novel, a method it shares with other modern tragicomedies.

CHAPTER TWENTY-TWO

Chapter twenty-two, physically in the center of *Catch-22*, provides us with much more detail on the two focal points of the novel: Snowden's death and Milo's syndicate operations.

As far as Snowden's death is concerned, we are given more information as to what happened and how, and this information is provided in such a way as to indicate how inter-connected the variety of things which "cause" his death are. This is important since the episode occurs within the context of the obvious dangers of war and is the major turning point for Yossarian since it was in this incident that "Yossarian lost his nerve." Appropriately, then, Heller re-introduces the image of the "trapped mouse," now symbolic of this aspect of the terrors besetting the men.

In the face of such obvious dangers, there would seem to be an obvious answer: direct action. So it is that Dobbs suggests that they kill Cathcart. (Note how Col. Cathcart is becoming the representative villain.) But the kind of intellectual clarity and singleness of purpose necessary for direct action are missing. Dobbs, too, has no individual perspective, no absolute conviction, and therefore must seek reassurances, which are not forthcoming for precisely the same reasons.

Suddenly, the chapter shifts its perspective. Using another reference to Orr's continual flight mishaps as the occasion, the chapter shifts in time and turns to an account, much fuller than we had before, of Milo's operations. Much of this account is comic, of course; we have, for instance, the woman procured by Milo and described in a parody of the old joke about a used car driven only on Sundays. But there is much here, even much that is funny in itself, that should alert the reader to deeper levels of meaning.

Age and time are here distorted, suggesting that, for everyone but Milo, time is psychological. (The reader can come to grips with such details by asking, "In whose eyes is this 32-year old an 'eighteen-year old virgin'?" And, what is the object of having someone describe her in this way?) Such distortions are accompanied by a consciousness that slurs over people falling and being trampled to death, and the whole scene is latent with tragedy even though it is comic on the surface.

Part of the effort of this presentation is to give us an idea of the interconnectedness of the syndicate, parallel to that shown regarding Snowden. Thus, here too, "everybody has a share." The syndicate, then, involves everyone, and it is also, though not so obviously, a threat. Or perhaps better put, it is a different kind of threat, one against which Dobb's proposal would be ineffectual even if carried out since everybody is involved. As Milo goes from place to place, the major here, the Caliph there, it becomes apparent that Milo is all the world and his syndicate "the way of all flesh." And, just as the trapped mouse symbolizes one sort of danger, so here the rain imagery symbolizes this danger.

CHAPTER TWENTY-THREE

The central concern of this chapter is the argument between Nately and the old man. Ranged around this core are the revelation of Aarfy's cruelty and the depiction of Nately's family, and all of this is set in the "apartment" in Rome. Thus we have Nately's world, both as it is and as he would have it be.

The argument itself revolves around Nately's cliches and the old man's sophistry. It deals principally with the meaning of strength and weakness, and these terms have to be defined in terms of one's desired end. For the old man, the end is simple: to stay alive. Therefore, principles have to go. Strength and sanity are measured only by survival, and whatever threatens survival must be rejected—for example, country and patriotism. And, indeed, if a country is no more than a body of land bounded arbitrarily, then why should one die for it? Thus, we have here again the theme of the value of one's life, the theme of sanity and madness, and the theme of appearance and reality.

But, the main point of the chapter seems to be Nately's inability to refute the old man. The old man is variously described as Satanic and diabolical, but Nately can't cope with his arguments. We only discover why at the end when we are made aware of how the old man reminds Nately of his father. Then we see, as Nately does not, that the only difference between this old man and Nately's father is a veneer. In spite of the contrast between the luxury of his home and the squalor of this tenement, both his family and the old man are hedonists at heart. Therefore, having no mind of his own, there is nothing in Nately's background to suggest an alternative to the old man's commitment to self-gratification. And, perhaps, we can't expect more of Nately in the face of such a formidable foe; after all, this is the same old man who could inflict a wound even upon Major — de Coverly.

CHAPTER TWENTY-FOUR

Again, we return to Milo: having established his operations earlier, we are now given a view of his character or thought processes. This presentation starts with a view of how his business not only overcomes nationality but also reaches beyond sides in the war. In consequence what belonged to the various nations becomes the property of the syndicate, displaying the syndicate name which ironically is painted over emblems symbolic of such traditional virtues as love, courage, etc.

Thus established, we can see the mentality necessary for such an operation. Milo presents a convenient variation on the lack of principles in the case of the old man: Milo has principles, but they are easily susceptible to rationalization. That is, as the old man represented the danger of pure unprincipledness, Milo represents the danger of unprincipledness masked so as to be publicly acceptable.

The upshot of Milo's "moral principles" is his refusal of responsibility for the bombing and strafing of his own squadron. In this regard, Milo, who refuses to acknowledge any personal responsibility, stands in direct contrast to the chaplain, who acknowledges total responsibility.

The one method of rationalization that Milo uses is the national security argument — anything can be justified if it promotes national security; this argument simply extends to the national survival the same rationale we have seen applied to individual survival throughout the novel. Another rationalization Milo uses is that he only wants to put things on the familiar "business-like basis"; translated: profit and loss become the sole arbiters of right and wrong.

Having suggested this "ethical" standard, it is appropriate that Milo meet Yossarian in a tree which Yossarian calls "the tree of life . . . and of knowledge of good and evil, too." This allusion to the Genesis story of the Fall is meant to confront us with the debasement of Milo's standard seen fully against the ethical background of our culture. Even Yossarian's nudity is an extension of the Genesis allusion.

The chapter is a model of structure as it mixes horror and comedy without stopping to draw distinctions between the two. Further, it adds more detail to the picture of Yossarian's post-Avignon nudity and gives us a picture of another side of Doc Daneeka's nature. In fact, Doc Daneeka's daring and commitment are here the absolute contrast to Milo's expediency, despite being given here as evidence that he has lost his head.

CHAPTER TWENTY-FIVE

Having portrayed Milo in Chapter 24, this chapter gives us a portrait of his opposite, the chaplain, a man we are told, "who had conscience and character." He is also a man torn between two poles, a tension which creates in him both skepticism and hope. On the one hand, there is the mystical chaplain who has visions and believes in the reality of some "spiritual epoch." Then there is the intellectual chaplain whose "mind was open on every subject," making him uncertain of everything.

There are, indeed, two "centers" in the chaplain's life, although Yossarian mistakes them for physical centers in his explanation of *deja vu,* "a momentary . . . lag in the operation of two coactive sensory nerve centers that commonly functioned together." The lag in the chaplain's case is between his intellectual life and his spiritual life. This is responsible for his sense of *deja vu,* and also for his sense that *deja vu, jamais vu, presque vu* are not "elastic enough" to cover the situation. In other words, we are back to the theme of an alternative way of seeing the world; and here we are given a view of one more condition, the chaplain's, which stands in the way of that alternative. Elasticity, incidentally, is a term Kierkegaard uses to characterize irony.

It is this gap, too, which accounts for his obsessive fears, for instance for his wife, and his sense, upon leaving Major Major's headquarters, of being chased by "peals of derisive laughter." Nevertheless, the chaplain has one sense which keeps him from being overcome by these fears and which offers hope of his coming to a new perception, and that sense is that "kindness and good manners" are more crucial than "complex questions of ontology." The chaplain needs, however, some view of things to justify that sense.

As we have seen earlier, the subject of *deja vu* is abetted by the structure of the book. Here, too, confused time schemes and the repetitious forms of argument, such as we have here between Col. Cathcart and Gen. Dreedle, create an almost *deja vu* phenomenon for the reader.

CHAPTER TWENTY-SIX

In this chapter, ranging through three episodes (the enlisted men's apartment, the "milk-run to Parma," and the hospital), Heller offers three pictures of insensitivity: Aarfy's insensitivity to Nately and his love, Aarfy's insensitivity to Yossarian at the time of his injury, and Dunbar's insensitivity in the game of pulling rank. Throughout, Nately and McWatt seem to be on the side of the angels, but note that Yossarian, who first falls into Aarfy's insensitivity by accident, is taking full part in Dunbar's game at the end. Thus the chapter again points up that Yossarian is a pivotal character and, in this case, gives him something like his just deserts. But the end result of experiencing terror and injury is not an increase in compassion, but a tendency toward callousness. Heller doesn't argue that this is true of necessity, but that is highly likely, a form of argument known in logic as *a fortiori;* thus the inclusion of a character whose name is a pun on this way of thinking, and whose place is taken by Yossarian.

This is a clue to the further process of the novel. It seems knowledge from the world (*a posteriori*) will not give answers to the novel's dilemma: not only are the perceptions of the world faulty, but, finally, all the world yields is "information"; and it seems that knowledge from first principles (*a priori*) is perhaps impossible and at least not in evidence: the chaplain has theological doubts, the Jehovan figure of Major — de Coverly seems now to be illusory, the ideals presented seem to be idiosyncrasies. But, the novel suggests, perhaps some of the dilemmas presented can be solved *a fortiori* — that is, on the basis of the best reasoning from the clearest sense of the nature of the situation.

CHAPTER TWENTY-SEVEN

Despite the vacillation in Yossarian's position which we have seen, he still has a better sense of reality than many people who confront him. We see this here in his sense that Nurse Duckett really needs people (as they all do) despite her facade. Nevertheless, Yossarian responds to that need in an exploitative manner.

His sexual assault on her is the occasion for the main story of this chapter, Yossarian's confrontation with the psychiatrist. As with most all of the comic episodes, this confrontation has a major thematic point. Along with the many jokes about Freudian psychology, the satire against psychiatry is carried on here by two main devices. First, there is the insistence of the psychiatrist on finding "the true reason" behind Yossarian's actions. That is, Sanderson can no more see reality than the chaplain can believe there really was a naked man in the tree. Both think there is a reality "behind" reality, and therefore neither can come to grips with the immediate reality of their lives.

Second, Heller transposes Gen. Dreedle's habit of mind — take him out and shoot him — to the psychiatrist. The point of the satire is precisely that the dilemma facing these men is not psychological in nature. And, in case we might forget what that problem is, Heller re-introduces Dobbs, who tells Yossarian, "I'm afraid to do anything alone." And this fear is not psychologically based. It is a deeper problem.

Throughout this episode, Heller interweaves another theme: the definition of reality. Here this theme revolves around Yossarian's sense of who he is versus Sanderson's identification of him as A. Fortiori, based on the "official" record. This misidentification results, of course, in A. Fortiori being sent home for Yossarian's behavior. This, in turn, leaves the supposedly crazy Yossarian to go back to war; and, once again, we have Catch-22 as Doc Daneeka asks, "Who else will go?"

CHAPTER TWENTY-EIGHT

Chapter 28 begins with the role reversal of Yossarian and Dobbs, a reversal which indicates not only the "Everyman" quality of each of them, but also how much each is subject to his own immediate circumstances and well-being. Into this context Orr is introduced; and, through a time shift, we see him "tinkering."

Orr tries to convince Yossarian that his continual ditching is "good practice," something of which Yossarian is decidedly not convinced. Note, however, that Orr will not tell Yossarian this directly. He only hints and Yossarian almost senses that Orr is trying to tell him something.

What stops Yossarian is not only that he can't imagine what ditching might be good practice for, but also that he has such ambiguous attitudes towards Orr himself. On the one hand, he regards him as brainless and worries about, "Who would protect him if he lived." Yossarian is concerned about Orr's innocence. On the other hand, we see enough of Orr to ask, who is really most able to cope? And, thinking of the severest threat to life, Yossarian himself thinks that "the idea of murdering Orr was so ridiculous." Thus this chapter suggests that perhaps the philosopher Kierkegaard was right: the best protection is innocence.

CHAPTER TWENTY-NINE

Having spent some time on General Dreedle's command, the novel now turns to General Peckem. (Together, one sees the humor in the names themselves.) And, as it does so, we find the paradox of an intense rivalry between the two commands. What makes the rivalry paradoxical is that essentially there is no difference between the two, and one is forced to ask, over what can there be a rivalry at all?

Perhaps, Heller means this to comment on the rivalry between nations, but there is a more immediate and substantial point. This point is suggested by the literary allusions to *Hamlet,* the drama of indecisiveness; for what follows our introduction to the Peckem-Scheisskopf-Cargill group is a progression of indecisiveness and rivalry.

Immediately after seeing the rivalry between Peckem and Dreedle, we see the rivalry, established by Gen. Peckem himself within his own command, between Cargill and Scheisskopf. In turn this rivalry passes over to that between the men in General Dreedle's command (for example, between Yossarian and Havermeyer). And this, in turn, passes over to the rivalry and indecision in one man — in this case, the familiar Col. Cathcart.

Whatever accounts for all of this, part of its explanation is the ambiguity created by the abuse of language, seen in the description of Gen. Peckem, and part comes from the tendency to accept as right whatever doesn't break the law (we have here rule by technicality).

For the most part, however, what contributes to the rivalry and indecision is a failure of the will. When Yossarian and others object to the proposed civilian bombing, they are asked the crucial question, "Would you rather go back to Bologna?" That is the question, as Hamlet said, to be or not to be?, or, translated to these terms, it is them or us. And, even among those who know it should not be "them," there is no one who will give himself up. And that is the final indecision, the final account for the rivalry.

CHAPTER THIRTY

This chapter begins with a change of mood and tone. In the descriptions of Dunbar, Yossarian, and McWatt we see a far more somber, serious, even desperate attitude and get the sense that things are beginning to come to a head. One evidence of this is seen in the changed regard for the issue of sanity and madness. Previously each of these characters had his own slant on what constituted sanity. Now, however, even Yossarian finds it impossible to determine about Dunbar whether he has seen "the light or scrambled his brains." Another evidence is found in the use of simile in the descriptions themselves; for instance, the description of the chaplain's tent is "like the cap of a tomb."

The chapter intentionally leaves us unclear as to what is responsible for this change. In keeping with the theme of perception as it has been developed, the change is made to seem less a result of previous events than an intuition of things to come. Therefore, what follows satisfies the conditions of an already somber, ominous beginning.

First we see the change in Yossarian as the playful thought of murdering Orr (seen earlier) becomes here at least a half-serious attempt to kill McWatt, whom, ironically, Yossarian had "scratched off" Dobb's assassination list. More important than the strangulation, however, is Yossarian's reaction to what he has done; "He was not angry anymore. He was ashamed," and we see him "hanging his head with guilt and remorse." And this is significant for it marks a change in Yossarian's self-perception from numbering himself at least potentially among the "victims" to counting himself as one of the perpetrators of evil. Yossarian is beginning to accept responsibility.

Imbedded in this account are the references to McWatt's playful buzzings of the tent, and this establishes the background for the final episode, the death of Kid Sampson. Again, ironically, the responsibility for this death is McWatt's, even though he is one of the "good guys" and had no malicious intent. But McWatt doesn't shrink from the responsibility, even for a moment; at least in terms of classical morality, he does the honorable thing. Thus he becomes the first person we see for whom living or continued existence doesn't come first.

Yet, there is one more dimension to this; for, however honorable McWatt's act is, it is called into question by Yossarian's call for McWatt, "to come down, McWatt, come down." Earlier, we could have read this as Yossarian's concern for "going on living"; following his own change, however, this has got to be taken as evidence of his as yet unarticulated sense of the meaning of life and responsibility. Thus Yossarian first senses what McWatt is going to do, sees that element of honor (he "dipped his wings once in salute"), but also sees an element of despair (he "decided oh, well, what the hell"). And he seems to feel that there must be an alternative to this.

CHAPTER THIRTY-ONE

Occasionally, we have followed the rapid time shift, but here we have a fairly chronological time sequence but a "rapid" shift in place. Doc Daneeka, really alive but "presumed dead," stands in stark contrast to Mudd, really dead but considered to be alive; and for this episode, the narrator switches us to "Mrs. Daneeka, Doc Daneeka's wife."

Ironically, the profit which Doc foresaw from the war comes true . . . but not for him. Mrs. Daneeka, grief-stricken "for about a full week," soon begins to realize a substantial profit from her husband's death; and, in consequence, her friends are relieved of "the obligation of continuous sympathy" which they resent.

By this point the novel is beginning to tie together some loose ends, so we have interwoven here the result of the clash between the chaplain and Sgt. Whitcomb: the form letter of condolences. More importantly, however, as these threads begin to come together into a tapestry, the image which has symbolized the most obvious threat of physical danger . . . the mouse . . . is here a metaphor for this less obvious threat of bureaucracy as Doc Daneeka begins to feel like an "ailing rodent."

CHAPTER THIRTY-TWO

The opening passages of this chapter depict Yossarian calling the roll of the dead, and his catalogue of the dead, the foolish, and the deluded reads like Ecclesiastes: "vanity, all is vanity." It is appropriate that this series of recollections leads to the re-introduction of the theme of mortality: "Death was irreversible, he suspected . . ."

In the face of his growing awareness of mortality, Yossarian grows closer to the memory of the now absent Orr, an identification prepared for by the indirect lure of Orr seen earlier. But, into the midst of this closeness, there arrive the new "roomies," whose exuberance clashes directly with Yossarian's gloom. Nevertheless, the chief thing noted about these young men is "their practical, direct efficiency," a quality which, the reader may see, as Yossarian does not, directly relates them to Orr. Thus between Yossarian, the "crotchety old foggy of twenty-eight," and these young roomies, "always in high spirits," there is a significant generation gap.

Note, too, that in the continuing effort to tie things up, we see in this brief chapter Doc Daneeka in the aftermath of his death, the reference to Yossarian's aversion to Black, and the continuing story of Chief White Halfoat.

CHAPTER THIRTY-THREE

As we get into this chapter, Yossarian both is in despair and having visions. The former picks up with Yossarian where we left off in the last episode relating the bombing of Ferrara, and the latter relates Yossarian even closer to the chaplain. This combination indicates a new stage in Yossarian's life, however painful, and shows that Yossarian is growing as a human being.

True to the novel's custom of counterpointing contrasts, this chapter turns next to the "middle-aged big shots" who are "utterly demoralized men of distinction." Of these men, the general is portrayed as a realist and a pragmatist. He is able to view the whole scene objectively, despite being involved. These qualities do set him apart from his compatriots; nevertheless, as positive as they are supposed to be, these same qualities do not stop him from exploiting human beings. In fact, his pragmatism and his brand of realism enable him to exploit, as we see when he delegates one of his "colleagues" to bring back their clothes.

Essentially, what happens in this episode is the first real, effectual reversal of the novel, as the "motley rescue party" from the squadron overcome the brass. They do so, first, through a reversal of the language games we have seen ("Your toes are dirty") and second, through forcefulness; and finally through Yossarian's attempt to lie, an attempt which, like the other two factors, aims at the psychology of demoralized men. The lie fails, at least with the general, and this indicates that, while the squad has won a battle, the war is yet to be fought.

Therefore, the chapter turns immediately to Nately and his whore. Despite all of his previous, calculated efforts, Nately finally "wins her heart" by something as simple as "a good night's sleep." But Nately is still playing the "Ivy league" role, while his girl is still habituated to her profession. In other words, the heroic stand has had its effect: love. But, all has not ended "happily ever after." Nately and his whore would still need a great change in character before this love could be realized. It is, though, a beginning: she really misses Nately (in contrast to the Yossarian we have just seen buying gifts for Nurse Duckett while trying to find Lucianna).

CHAPTER THIRTY-FOUR

The opening descriptions of the Thanksgiving party show decadence, a la ancient Rome, as the end result of, on the one hand, the rampant hedonism of these men and, on the other hand, the desperation of men trying to escape their circumstances with some kind of sanity.

This latter aspect is emphasized by Yossarian's own outraged attack on the machine gun nest and, in the course of things, on Nately. And, note, that Yossarian's own reaction to this is less remorseful than before.

The party scene sets the stage for the return to the hospital, and by now it has become an almost universal refuge. We even find the chaplain there in somewhat ambiguous circumstances. He "had sinned, and it was good." Nevertheless, the narrator is quite candid in saying that this "sin" was like all others, a result of "protective rationalization," or more sternly, a result of having "no character." This episode is essential to the chaplain's growth in the same way as Yossarian's brutal attack on McWatt was essential. The chaplain has always regarded "sin" as being "out there" and thus felt helpless in the face of it. Before he can come to a sense of mastery, he must first see sin as being "in here," a part of him. And for that the chaplain must sin, and so he does. It is the beginning of the chaplain's attempt to come to terms with reality.

But the hospital scene is itself just the means to another issue. This issue begins with the return of "the soldier in white." This time, there is a notable speculation that "There's no one inside," a testimony false on its factual level—Lt. Schmulker is "inside"—but carrying thematic overtones concerning what, if anything, exists as far as the inner man is concerned. The idea, however, catches on and prepares the way for the real subject:

the idea of "disappearing" people and the theme of the disappearance of the individual.

CHAPTER THIRTY-FIVE

With chapter thirty-five, the satire is becoming more obvious, both in terms of the identification of the realms satirized (Milo's mentality and its effect on the number of missions) and in terms of the blatant abuse of sense being perpetrated on all sides. Thus, for example, the earlier slogan, "everyone has a share," is here advanced to the obvious mockery of "what's fair is fair" and to Milo's covering philosophy, "the historic right of free men to pay as much as they had to for the things they needed in order to survive."

How really trite all of the Milo/Cathcart business has become is pointed out by the puns imbedded in Milo's catalogue of business affairs – for example, the Cedars of Lebanon and the coals at Newcastle. And these puns point also to the idea that Milo has learned the artifacts of his culture without making that culture itself a part of him. It is also important to note who convinces whom in this dialogue.

One response to this nearly grotesque exaggeration of affairs would be laughter; the only way to cope is to have a sense of humor. And this response is not only recommended by common wisdom but also has been seen before as a somewhat effective means employed by the men of the squadron. This chapter rules out that response immediately. No sooner have we seen Milo's chicanery than do we see the result: raising the number of missions; and this time, the numbers aren't just abstract. Dobbs is killed, and "Nately, in the other plane, was killed too."

CHAPTER THIRTY-SIX

At the death of Nately, the chaplain instinctively prays. Usually for prayer to be instinctive would demean prayer, but for the chaplain, usually abstract, it is a real step in his getting in touch with himself. We notice, in this regard, that the chaplain is beginning to identify his fears. This ability to "name" one's fears is the opposite of despair, the quality we see in Yossarian as he lands. And in Yossarian's case we see this despair as a result of the ever-growing consciousness of mortality, seen in Yossarian's earlier sense of death and abetted here by Nately's death.

The chapter moves immediately to the interrogation of the chaplain. This interrogation is, except for Yossarian's security clearance later, the last of a series of trials and investigations throughout the novel, emphasizing how important the theme of law and "illegal legality" is in the novel. First, we see two apparently different personalities, one hard-nosed and the other conciliatory. But we see what comes of the conciliatory attitude as the more easy going of the two ultimately parrots the same line as his coarser colleague. Next, we see the same kind of language game as we have seen before being used to confuse the issue in the chaplain's interrogation. This game emphasizes the mentality at work here: if we are questioning you, you must be guilty. True to this line of thought, the interrogating officers wear no insignia: they are the personification of this warped logic, and, thus too, they have no names.

They have an effect on the chaplain, however, as does their "named" counterpart, Col. Korn, because the chaplain does "feel" guilty in general. He is faced, therefore, with the conflict between mere instinct and "immoral logic." What we have here is a miniature "descent into hell." The novel will pick up on this literary device later.

CHAPTER THIRTY-SEVEN

Peckem's plans fall apart in an ironic twist: his own machinations are his undoing. Moreover, Scheisskopf becomes the general in charge, and, of course, orders parades. But here, the order is expressly for *"everybody to march,"* words with quite a different connotation than the word "parade."

Heller has set this brief chapter aside for a symbolic purpose: worldly wisdom (cleverness) fails—absolute conformity reigns—and the way for this reign was paved precisely by that very cleverness which, through arbitrary caprice, sought to control the spirit of men.

CHAPTER THIRTY-EIGHT

As this chapter begins, we find that a real change has occurred in Yossarian. Some would say he is paranoid, but paranoia means "unreasonable fear" and Yossarian's fear is really a wholly merited distrust of the world. All of this is the reason for his refusal to fly more missions, and this refusal prompts another literary allusion as Col. Korn compares Yossarian to Achilles. In *The Iliad* Achilles refuses to fight, only coming into the battle when his friend is killed; this happens only when the battle touches upon him and his sense of right and wrong and thus, one of its purposes is to define honor. Thus, through this allusion, Yossarian, as a character, is related to the core of Western ideas about life and honor.

Following this beginning we are given a flashback to one of the principle causes of Yossarian's change, not only Nately's death but its effect on his "whore." In this episode we see how differently grief can affect people and also how close love and hate can become in the context of grief. This is, in its way, a study in the complexity of human emotions as well as a story of subterfuge. As Nately's whore begins to appear everywhere, we begin to see that she symbolizes Yossarian's guilty conscience, an apt response to his claim, "I didn't kill him."

Now Yossarian has refused to fly, and his decision is contagious. Soon he is overwhelmed with compatriots who are taking a new interest in him. And Appleby's reference to his heroism is now true: he has finally behaved heroically, with some idea of the consequences to him but also with a disregard for himself. Suddenly he is made aware of a human bond "he had not guessed." His new-found conviction is changing his perception of the world, the major theme of the novel.

As evidence of this we have the subtle touch that the squadron is still referred to as Dunbar's even though Dunbar has "disappeared." But more directly we have the new revelations which appear during his conversations. First, with Appleby, it is driven home that the reality of death orders our sense of proportion: "Now that he's dead, I guess it doesn't matter any more whether I'm a better ping-pong player or not." And, having already seen the impact of death on human lives and relationships (Nately's whore), it comes as no surprise that an awareness of death is a potent spiritual force.

Second, with Havermeyer we find what really "forces" these men to acquiesce: "You get five hundred dollars a year if you stay in the reserves." That is, they are motivated only by their own paltriness and materialistic urges. And this is pointed up by the fact that Yossarian's decision and its contagion have come too late to save Nately and his whore and his whore's kid sister. They perish because of his paltriness, thus the whore is a fitting image for his guilty conscience. And the image of their perishing is true to the disregard for the individual human life which paltriness abets; they are "flushed right out into the street."

CHAPTER THIRTY-NINE

Having found that the girls are on the streets, along with all humanity, Yossarian plunges into the streets, too. This plunge is characterized as an exercise of his freedom and independence, only words to most but realities to Yossarian. And Yossarian sees them as realities because he is willing to act. Having found himself a culprit and not just a victim, he now sees that this is universally true of mankind — true of all those who will not refuse to be either.

This same idea comes out in the visit to the old woman, as Yossarian realizes that Catch-22 doesn't really exist. It only exists so long as people, fearful for themselves as this old woman is fearful, allow might to make right — part of the real philosophy encountered in *Catch-22*.

Having learned this, the question arises as to whether Yossarian will be true to what he knows. How will Yossarian understand his new knowledge? Will he maintain his sense of possible triumph only by putting on rose-colored glasses? Or, will he allow a realistic view of his world to undermine that sense?

To begin to determine the answer to these questions Heller includes the episode of Yossarian's journey through Rome and the episode of Aarfy's crime. As far as the journey is concerned, there are two things to note.

First, the journey is not realistic, but, as we are told, "surrealistic"; it takes place in another reality, and for this Heller makes use of a traditional literary form called "the descent into hell" (or "the night journey"). This descent is prepared for by the many passing references to specters, etc. In the literary tradition, heroes descended to the place of the dead for several reasons and at least three are operating here. Like Orpheus descending to rescue Euridice, Yossarian goes to rescue Nately's whore's kid sister. Like Aeneas or Ulysses descending to find knowledge, Yossarian sees what the world is like. And like various figures who descend for healing, Yossarian descends as a man whose "spirit was sick." That this is a "descent" pattern is attested to by all sorts of details: it occurs in Rome; it is cold, dark, and "tomb-like," the shadow-like figures "materialize," and he walks through streets of teeth reminiscent of the valley of dry bones. Even, explicitly, however, Yossarian speaks of the warning call he hears as a "heroic warning from the grave." In other words, by using this tradition, Heller has sent Yossarian on the heroic path and we will see whether or not he emerges as did the heroes.

Second, Heller interweaves another literary tradition here. The descent is prefaced by Yossarian's thoughts of the suffering of children, thoughts precisely reminiscent of Ivan's in Dostoevsky's *Brothers Karamazov*. And during the descent there is a major allusion to Raskolnikov, the protagonist in Dostoevsky's *Crime and Punishment*.

The reference to Ivan is a prelude to Yossarian's exclamation, "What a lousy earth," an echo of Ivan himself. Thus Yossarian sees all the horror and hurt the world is capable of, culminating in the idea that "mobs . . . were in control everywhere." Mob rule is all we can expect in a Catch-22 world where, ultimately, might makes right; and Yossarian must not gloss over this reality into blissful optimism. But, Ivan is overcome by this view and this raises the question of its effect on Yossarian.

Here is where the reference to Raskolnikov comes in; for, unlike Ivan, Raskolnikov, himself a base criminal, is led to see that the evil of the world is within. So, in sequence, we have the allusion to Raskolnikov's dream of suffering. Then Yossarian, observing all of this, identifies himself with Christ. Then we have Yossarian's experience of *deja vu,* an experience from which Yossarian "recoiled with sickening recognition." As a psychic phenomenon, that recognition is of the "scene he had witnessed a block before." But, as we have seen, *deja vu* in this novel describes an internal discrepancy between intellect and spirit; and what Yossarian sickenly recognizes is himself in the "immobile crowd of adult spectators who made no effort to intervene" just as, in the scene a block earlier, "Yossarian quickened his pace to get away." That is the end of his identification with Christ—who like a doctor walks through the ward of the world—and the beginning of his sense that it is "his spirit" which is "sick."

The nature of this sickness is seen in the change which has come over Yossarian. He had started his "descent" full of purpose, a direct contrast with Milo who is turned aside by material concerns. But now he wishes to retreat into that naturalistic world of sensuality which, along with the hospital, has been his "escape" before.

This time the retreat takes him face-to-face with Aarfy's crime, a crime of sensuality. And this episode ends with Yossarian the ironic victim of Catch-22. That is, this chapter has ended by putting Yossarian in the position of victim, by putting him to the test so far as his new-found knowledge of how to triumph over Catch-22 is concerned. And the way for this test has been prepared by the descent episode and the scene of Aarfy's crime.

The title of this chapter may well refer to a painting by Peter Blume of the same name, done in 1934-37; and readers will get a visual sense of the vandalized condition described in this chapter if they study this painting.

CHAPTER FORTY

As chapter thirty-nine closed, Yossarian first became the victim of an ironic arrest and then was given hope of a reprieve, of being sent home. In chapter forty, we find, however, that there is a catch. Here in this, the title chapter, Catch-22 reasserts itself.

Yossarian's refusal to fly more missions has evidently given the men hope, has suggested that there is an alternative. This has created a problem for Korn and Cathcart, a problem which threatens the achievement of their ambitions for promotion. Their solution is, of course, ingenious: send Yossarian home, but with just one little catch—he is to go home "a friend."

Note that they first try to get Yossarian to change his mind by appealing to his patriotism. Yossarian, however, refuses to make the false identification of Cathcart and Korn with his country. Yossarian's patriotism is to the country, not to these men. When this approach fails, they appeal to Yossarian to accept the deal; and this appeal is to his desire for safety, on the one hand, and to "reason" on the other. Against safety and a "privileged existence" are the ideas that the deal will "offend your conscience" and the idea of "moral principle"; and the "sensible move" is to accept the deal.

And, as we read, we find Yossarian, finding "no reason . . . to risk my life for them," makes the sensible move. There are two consequences, however, to be noted. The first is the most subtle of the two. In the appeals to Yossarian, he is accused of being "calculating," of refusing to fly in order to get sent home, of refusing out of self-interest. Yossarian denies this, and in retrospect his denial is true: when he refused to fly he had no idea what the consequences would be. But by entering into this deal, his denial becomes false. It ultimately becomes a matter of calculation; and, therefore, what was a simple refusal becomes "an act of rebellion," an act which Yossarian is now measuring only in terms of its success. Yossarian's distinction between the two colonels and his country has ironic force as his serving the ends of the colonels leads him into a disservice to his country.

The second thing to note, while not so subtle, is of equal importance: although Yossarian has capitulated—and it is through his own weakness that Catch-22 re-asserts itself—the story is not over. The capitulation does offend his conscience as we discover when Nately's whore, symbolic of his guilty conscience, attacks him just as he leaves Col. Korn and Col. Cathcart.

CHAPTER FORTY-ONE

At the beginning of this chapter, we find Yossarian's supposedly sensible move called into question by the fact that one consequence of that move is his landing in the hospital in a "fog of insensibility." Also, it is fitting that, as the story began in the hospital, it end there, too. Knowing what we now do about the novel's structure, it should not surprise us if, just as the first chapter set the scene for the rest of the story, something like that would happen here. And so it does in three major ways.

The first of these can be seen in Yossarian's answer to the interrogation in the hospital. "Where were you born?" he is asked. "On a battlefield . . . in a state of innocence," he replies. There is more here than just the literal sense that Yossarian became a new man in the experience of the war. Such broad, metaphoric replies are intended to convey a truth about the human condition. The truth conveyed here is decidedly Miltonic, both in metaphor and in substance, and represents, in the inclusion of the concept of innocence, a spiritual sense of life.

Second, having placed himself in this tradition and perspective, Yossarian encounters the strange man who claims to have Yossarian's pal, a claim Yossarian frankly doesn't understand. In trying to understand, Yossarian keeps asking, over and over, "who's my pal?" The sheer repetition of the question suggests its biblical parallel, who is my neighbor?, the question which prompted Christ's parable of the Good Samaritan.

Third, because the parable raises the idea of one's neighbor (pal) beyond the idea of "a friend" (and because of the cold), Yossarian thinks of the most vivid case he knows of a man in need who, nevertheless, "had never been his pal" but only "a vaguely familiar kid": Snowden. And it is as if, for most of the novel, it has been Snowden and his secret (what Snowden's case represents) that have dominated Yossarian's thinking and been the motivating factor in his fearful quest for survival.

As we are told the whole, gruesome story of Snowden's death, his "secret" is revealed to us as it had once, in Yossarian's presence, "spilled all over the messy floor." "Man was matter, that was Snowden's secret." And the conclusion to be drawn from this view is plain, "Ripeness is all." This is the view that has set Yossarian on the path he has pursued through most of the novel, the view referred to in the note to chapter six as *carpe diem*. And certainly we can understand how such a vivid incident could unconsciously influence a man. But, the view is qualified: "The spirit gone, man is garbage." You cannot be a "pal" to garbage. With Yossarian, however, his concern for "who's my pal" and his spiritual definition of life suggest that the spirit is not or need not be gone. And with spirit, what then?

CHAPTER FORTY-TWO

The most important definition in the novel is given by Yossarian as he tells Danby the deal is off, and this is his definition of weakness as the desire "to save my life."

Confronted in this belief by Danby, Yossarian finds Danby-the-man on the one side and the ideas Danby expresses on the other. Danby, the self-admitted coward, must be rejected as a model. But what Danby says, particularly about not letting the difference between men and ideals stop one from regarding the welfare of his country and the dignity of man, must be accepted. For this to take place, Yossarian has to clarify how he regards himself; and the ideals Danby speaks of must cease to seem abstract.

One can see this work out by following the progression of Yossarian's thoughts. At first, contemptuous of Danby and frustrated by the "Scheisskopfs, Peckems, Korns, and Cathcarts," Yossarian talks of saving himself. "I'm going to fight a little to save myself. The country's not in danger anymore, but I am." But as Yossarian pursues this reasoning, he comes to the *deja vu* recognition. He sees this as the line of thought he had pursued all along until he realized its weakness. Having been brought to his senses he can tell Danby that what Danby considers "a way to save yourself" is really "a way to lose myself." From here on out, saving oneself will take on the new meaning of not dissipating one's energies, as the chaplain did (praying "takes my mind off my troubles . . . And it gives me something to do") and as Col. Korn and Col. Cathcart do (who want promotion because, "What else have we got to do?"). In other words, it means being willing to risk oneself to save oneself for something higher.

This sense gives Yossarian courage, the "courage to defy somebody" (note: to defy somebody, not to rebel). At this point, however, it seems that the situation is hopeless. That is, doomed to failure in material terms, all the courageous man can do is live with "all these crushing burdens" in a kind of infinite resignation. But hope immediately enters the picture with the story of Orr. His name itself makes him the symbol of some alternative and is also a pun on "oar"—the point being that Orr was not "up a creek without a paddle."

Orr and his "miracle" now replace Snowden and his death as the model for and influence on Yossarian's thinking. The miracle shows Yossarian what tremendous potential men have for "intelligence," "endurance," and "perseverance." The immediate consequence of this newfound hope, this faith in man, is that Yossarian now sees the concreteness of the dignity of man which Danby had mentioned. This frees Yossarian from sentimentality about "people cashing in on every decent impulse and every human tragedy." Possessed by a belief in human possibility, Yossarian can forget about the men who obscure the ideals; "Let the bastards thrive . . . since I can't do a thing to stop them . . . I've got responsibilities of my own."

And this new belief is not the moral idealism of Danby's either. Yossarian knows well enough how easily human nature can mask "saving oneself" as the "sensible move." And so he says of his conscience, "God bless it . . . I wouldn't want to live without strong misgivings." And, as Yossarian jumps away from Nately's whore, from his own sense of guilt, he runs with hope and courage to his responsibilities.

This example rejuvenates the chaplain, too. But note that rejuvenation and hope do not dictate "going to Sweden." For the chaplain it means, "I'll stay here and persevere." In other words, we end with the idea that the chaplain expressed earlier, "you must do whatever you think is right." Now, however, the emphasis is on the "must do" rather than on "whatever you think," as it was earlier. And with this new emphasis, whether it means staying or leaving, Catch-22 is defeated.

THE NOVEL AND ITS TRADITIONS

By one means or another a serious writer associates his work with certain literary traditions which have spoken eloquently to the issues and ideas which he tries to portray. This is certainly true of *Catch-22,* where explicit allusions and adoptions of particular genres make it clear that Heller has certain traditions and perspectives in mind. But these traditions are manifold and bear drawing out.

The first of these, or the most obvious, is the tradition of satire. (Satire is a step-son of tragedy, the difference between the two being that tragedy deals with a fall from moral dignity while satire deals with a departure from moral rules. The former is subjective; the latter, objective and "codifiable.") In this vein, the novel takes hypocrisy, bureaucracy, and the "sins of wealth" to task. But satire must always imply a standard which is upheld by the depiction of its being forsaken. And here the standard seems to be the individual and what is satirized is whatever threatens to destroy the individual. In this regard *Catch-22* represents a departure from the social protest of earlier, "proletarian" writers who concentrated on the masses and on social reform.

This reference to the individual, however, goes through many faltering stages. One of these stages, that encompassing Yossarian's rebellion and decision not to be brave, trades on a more recent tradition of the anti-hero in general and the anti-war novel in particular. This tradition includes Remarque's *All Quiet on the Western Front,* Hasek's *The Good Soldier Schweik,* and Hemingway's *A Farewell to Arms* (as well as Crane and Mailer). The solidarity of this tradition, however, is very ephemeral. The protagonists in this tradition do learn that the reality of war is far different from slogans and oratory about war. But their response to this new awareness and their development from that point as characters take very different forms. Considering Schweik, who always looks out for himself, usually in the guise of some subterfuge, as the anti-heroic model, *Catch-22* can be considered part of this tradition only in its preparatory or initial stages (which do, however, cover most of the course of the novel). Militating against this tradition are explicit elements; for example, Yossarian's defense of his patriotism, and implicit themes regarding the inadequacy of the unheroic approach to life. Combining these first two traditions, some of the people satirized are more perfect types of anti-hero than is Yossarian, even in the beginning. (*Catch-22* bears more resemblance to *A Farewell to Arms,* which also falls out of the tradition in terms of the comment made on its hero's development.)

What gives rise to identification with this tradition is another closely allied tradition, that of the absurd. *Catch-22* does share much with this perspective, a perspective fostered by such authors as Camus, Sartre, and Kafka. Among other things, the emphasis on the individual, the attention to an "irrefutable" bureaucracy, and the general pursuit of irrelevance in the face of a lack of accepted general principles bear out this identification. This identification, too, can only go so far. For one thing, when treated as an absurdist novel, most critics find *Catch-22* falls short. Since it is on other grounds, a fine novel, this should indicate not that it fails in that category but that it doesn't fit into that category. For another thing, once again, those who most pursue irrelevance, for example, are also those satirized.

What makes absurdism attractive is its roots. Absurdism is born of two traditions. First, there is the classical tradition wherein the hero had to make sense of the world, if he could, out of the materials of his own struggles rather than from the way his world presented itself. Second, there is the existential tradition, wherein the hero casts off preconceptions and moral idealism either for despair or for moral realism. And it is these two sources which inform *Catch-22*.

On the one hand, in its use of devices from Greek drama and of one of the chief classical conventions, the descent or night journey, *Catch-22* identifies itself with the classics. On the other hand, in its allusions or settings from Schopenhauer, Nietzsche, and Dostoevsky (as well as Camus and Tolstoy), in its use of bureaucracy as a metaphor, and in its insistence on casting off sentimentality, the novel falls into the existential tradition.

With the classical tradition it shares a vision of a hero developed through error, suffering, and enlightenment. With the existential tradition it shares a spiritual view of a man who finds or loses himself in the unpremeditated "leap" of allegiance to something higher (or lower) than himself.

A reader familiar with these traditions will be better able to read *Catch-22*; and, conversely, a reader of *Catch-22* is led back to these traditions.

QUESTIONS FOR REVIEW

1. Describe in detail the progression of Yossarian from escapism to courage and responsibility.
2. Does the chaplain have a function in the novel? How does he relate to the men, the issues, and himself?
3. What relation does the novel suggest exists between vice and boredom? How does it account for this boredom?
4. What does the novel portray as the consequences of self-protection? of risk?
5. What role does time play in both the structure and the themes of the novel?
6. Discuss Pianosa both as setting and as metaphor.
7. Explain how the hospital in Pianosa and the apartment in Rome function in the novel.
8. Why does Major——de Coverly disappear from the novel midway in its course?
9. Discuss the role played by literary allusion in the novel.
10. Trace the development of M&M Enterprises and its effect on the lives of the men.
11. Describe one of the repeated events in the novel and indicate what this repetition contributes to plot and theme.
12. What function is fulfilled by the presence of many characters named only by description (for example, the soldier in white, the maid in the lime-colored panties)?
13. Describe how humor and terror, comedy and tragedy are interwoven in the novel.

14. What are the various levels of rivalry in the novel, and what accounts for each level?
15. Discuss the war and the military as metaphors and, also, why this arena can serve as such a metaphor.
16. Outline the various perspectives on life and death and detail which characters represent each perspective.

SELECTED BIBLIOGRAPHY

Castelli, Jim. "*Catch-22* and the New Hero." *Catholic World.* 211: 199-202.

Deniston, Constance. "The American Romance Parody," *Emporia State Research Studies.* 14, ii (1965): 42-59.

Doskow, Minna. "The Night Journey," *Twentieth Century Literature.* 12: 186-93.

French, Michael. "The American Novel in the Sixties," *Midwest Quarterly.* 9: 365-79.

Gaukroger, Doug. "Time Structure in *Catch-22*," *Critique: Studies in Modern Fiction.* 12, ii: 70-85.

Hunt, John W. "Comic Escape and Anti-Vision," in Nathan Scott, *Adversity and Grace: Studies in Recent American Literature.* Chicago: University of Chicago Press, 1968.

Leham, Richard and Jerry Patch. "*Catch-22*: The Making of a Novel," *Minnesota Review.* VII (1967), 238-44.

Levine, Edward. "The Inflated Image: Satire and Meaning in Pop Art," *Satire Newsletter.* 6, i: 43-50.

McNamara, Eugene. "The Absurd Style in Contemporary American Literature," *Humanities Association Bulletin.* 19,i: 44-49.

Mellard, James W. "*Catch-22: Deja Vu* and the Labyrinth of Memory," *Bucknell Review.* 16, ii: 29-44.

Milne, Victor J. "Heller's 'Bologniad': A Theological Perspective on *Catch-22*," *Critique: Studies in Modern Fiction.* 12, ii: 50-69.

Muste, John W. "Better to Die Laughing," *Critique: Studies in Modern Fiction.* 5, ii: 16-27.

Pinsker, Sanford. "Heller's *Catch-22*: The Protest of a Puer Eternis," *Critique: Studies in Modern Fiction.* 7, ii: 150-62.

Solomon, Jan. "The Structure of Joseph Heller's *Catch-22*," *Critique: Studies in Modern Fiction.* 12, ii: 50-69.

Stern, J. P. "War and the Comic Muse: *The Good Soldier Schweik* and *Catch-22*," *Comparative Literature.* 20: 193-216.

Thomas, W. K. " 'What Difference Does It Make?' Logic in *Catch-22*," *Dalhousie Review.* 50: 488-95.

Waldmeir, Joseph. "Two Novelists of the Absurd: Heller and Kesey," *Wisconsin Studies in Contemporary Literature.* 5 (1964): 192-204.

Wain, John. "A New Novel About Old Troubles," *Critical Quarterly.* 5: 168-73.

Way, Brian. "Formal Experiment and Social Discontent: Joseph Heller's *Catch-22*," *Journal of American Studies.* 2: 253-70.